# The *Tabernacle*

## Entering into God's Presence

Ian Sewter

Published 2002 by CWR, Waverley Abbey House, Waverley Lane,
Farnham, Surrey GU9 8EP, England, UK.



See back of book for list of National Distributors.



Concept development, editing, design and production by CWR.
Front cover image: Roger Walker.
Printed by Linney Print.

ISBN 1-85345-230-0

## Contents

# Introduction

God has always desired to dwell with His people. We see in Genesis 3:8 that He walked in the Garden of Eden to enjoy an intimate relationship with Adam and Eve. Their sin produced a barrier to that relationship and a separation of the Creator from His creation. It was no longer possible for God and man to meet together in intimacy, until the building of the tabernacle, which provided a place where God's holiness could reside in an unholy world. It was effectively the "meeting point" of heaven and earth.

It has been said that there is more written in the Bible about the tabernacle than any other subject. Fifty chapters in the Old and New Testaments are devoted to its construction and meaning and yet it is a subject that is largely ignored among Christians today. The tabernacle is a prime example of what is referred to as the typology of Scripture. Bible places, events and people are recognised as types when they are seen to prefigure or prophesy a subsequent event. In addition, parts of the New Testament can only be understood by reference to the Old Testament type. For example, when John the Baptist spoke of Jesus as the "Lamb of God, who takes away the sin of the world" (John 1:29), he was referring to the practice of sacrifices offered in the tabernacle to obtain forgiveness for sin (Lev. 5:1–6:7). The sacrificial lamb without blemish, was a type of Christ, who would give His life as a guilt offering for the sin of the world.

The word "tabernacle" simply means, "dwelling place". The tabernacle itself was a movable structure where God dwelt among the Israelites who were encamped around it. It consisted of an outer court and, towards the far end, a large tent. The first section of the tent was the Holy Place and was only accessible by the priests. A thick curtain called the veil stretched across the inside of the tent and separated the Holy of Holies where only the high priest was allowed, once a year, on the Day of Atonement. The importance of the tabernacle for Christians is emphasised in the New Testament book of Hebrews, which explains how and why guilty sinners can experience an intimate relationship with a holy God. The tabernacle was laid out in such a way that it symbolises the path to relationship, then friendship and, finally, intimacy with God. It speaks very clearly of Jesus. For example, there were three entrances to the tabernacle. The entrance to the outer court was called the gate, the entrance to the Holy Place was called the door and the entrance to the Holy of Holies was the veil. Jesus is the way (John 14:6), the gate that we must pass through (John 10:9) and his flesh the veil rent in two when he gave up His spirit (Heb. 10:19–20; Matt. 27:51). Much of the book of Hebrews explores and explains the Old Testament sacrificial system and how Jesus' sacrifice, once and for all, both consummated and made that system obsolete – cleansing us by His blood from all sin and giving us access to the throne of God's mercy.

In this respect it is vital to note that the tabernacle was not Moses' idea but God's! It was not the product of human whim or imagination but fundamental to the plan and purposes of God. Exodus 25:8 records, "I want the people of Israel to build me a sacred residence where I can live among them" (NLT). Furthermore, it was specifically built following God's detailed designs; verse 9: "You must make this Tabernacle and its furnishings exactly according to the plans I will show you" (NLT). It is those plans that are the subject of this short study. As you read about the tabernacle, the priests and the offerings, always keep in mind that they speak about Jesus and are foundational in our understanding of why He had to die to save us from the consequences of our sin. Our understanding of that truth will lead us into spiritual freedom, peace and joy as we come to experience God dwelling in us as He once dwelt in the tabernacle!

**Note:** Some Bible translations use different words to describe the same item, e.g. the veil is simply referred to as curtain in the NIV.

WEEK 1

# Preparing to Build

## Opening Icebreaker

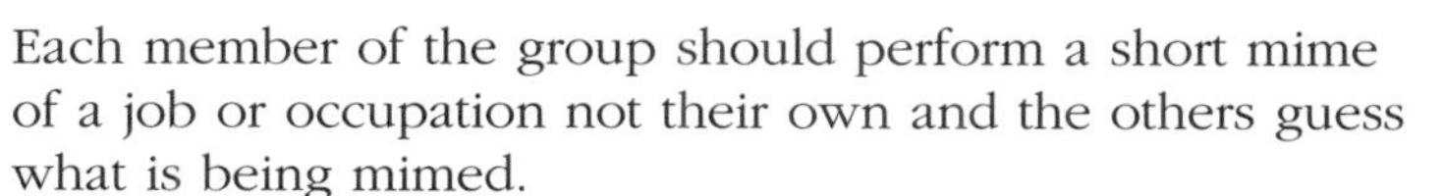

Each member of the group should perform a short mime of a job or occupation not their own and the others guess what is being mimed.

## Bible Readings

- Exodus 35:4–36:7
- Romans 12:4–8
- 1 Corinthians 12:12–31

## Opening Our Eyes

In order to make anything – from a cup of tea to a modern skyscraper – we need the same basic elements: raw materials and human effort. Add to these skill, knowledge, tools and plans and we can reach even beyond the sky and send our spacecraft to other planets! Include God's wisdom and power and nothing will be impossible! Preparation is the key to fruitful lives and successful projects. The ministry of John the Baptist was to "prepare the way for the Lord" (Matt. 3:1–3). It was John's preaching that forged a message of repentance and righteousness throughout Israel and created an expectation in people's hearts of the coming of the Messiah (Mark 1:7–8; John 1:35–37).

Preparation is the key to our own lives and to the ministry of the Church. Early missionaries first prepared themselves in their own countries by learning strange languages, eating unusual foods and sleeping on hard floors before travelling overseas, so they could more effectively share the gospel in a different culture. As individuals we have natural talents, learned abilities and gifts provided supernaturally by God. Many of us also possess houses, books, cars and bank accounts. In 1 Chronicles 29:14, King David acknowledges to God that, "Everything we have has come from you, and we only give you what is yours already" (TLB).

The story of the construction of the tabernacle starts when everyone with a willing heart brought gold, silver, skins, olive oil, cloth and precious stones. The tabernacle and all its furnishings were to be constructed of the most costly of materials and the people were called to be sacrificial in their giving. The best of all that the community had to offer was literally poured into the project. Skilled men and women took these materials and turned them into a supernatural place where God could live among His people. Both the materials out of which the tabernacle would be constructed and their labour were to be given freely, as a freewill offering, to symbolise that they desired their God to make His habitation among them. The story ends with the completion of the tabernacle and the power and majesty of an omnipotent and omnipresent God filling it with His awesome glorious presence (Exod. 40:34–35)!

The New Testament Church is built in exactly the same way. We are disciples in training to be fruitful and productive in the kingdom of God. We join with other believers as living stones to be built into a holy temple that God can inhabit (1 Pet. 2:5). Each of us has special abilities and can contribute to building up the Body of Christ in love. Research has indicated that the average person has around 600 skills! We may not be a powerful preacher but we can offer a stranger a warm welcome and a cup of tea. Some of us may be good with figures and prepare church accounts, or type a newsletter, play an instrument or help in the crèche so a young mother can attend an evangelistic meeting. As we prove to be faithful servants, God will often give us new abilities and widen our responsibilities. We are the raw material that God uses to build His Church, with Christ Himself as the foundation and cornerstone. If God can make a beautiful world out of chaos, and humanity from a speck of dust, there can be no limit to what He can create from the life that is dedicated to Him! As the people of God give the resources of God, to the ministers of God, for the work of God, He will know that He is welcome among us. Our lives and churches will be filled with the glorious presence of God. Hallelujah!!

Let us offer ourselves, our abilities and our possessions to the greatest Architect and Builder of all.

## Discussion Starters

1. How can we show God that He is welcome among us?

2. How important was an inspiring vision in motivating God's people to construct the tabernacle? How clear is your vision for your own life/church?

3. What training/help do you need to develop skills in order to be more spiritually fruitful?

4. What does it mean to "prepare the way of the Lord" and how are you preparing the way for the Lord in your own life?

5. The building of the tabernacle was costly and involved sacrificial giving. How effectively do you think you use your time, talents and treasures in the building of the Church?

6. How can we strike the right balance between commitments to work, church, family, friends and relaxation?

7. What causes you to waste your abilities and how can you change?

8. What are the different roles and responsibilities of God and man in building the Church?

9. It is important for the building of the Church that we affirm the contributions made by others. What gifts and positive characteristics do you see in other members of your group?

## Personal Application

As members of the Body of Christ we all have a role to fulfil to enrich the whole. The Church is only built where people willingly and freely offer themselves and their possessions to God for Him to use. We can prepare ourselves by prayer, reading the Bible, fellowshipping with other believers and enrolling on courses to develop our natural and supernatural gifts. We also have to work together in harmony, each of us using our different abilities for the common purpose. We may be a multimillionaire, a boy with a few loaves and fish or a widow with two coins. We may be single, newly married, raising children or elderly, simply serving the Lord in prayer (Luke 2:36–38), but we all have a vital contribution to building up Christ's Body here on earth. The Church is enriched by our contributions and impoverished by our lack of involvement.

## Seeing Jesus in the Scriptures

Jesus offered Himself as a servant without reservation to fulfil the purposes of God, even though it cost Him His life. His obedience to God was not based on duty but on delight to do God's will. He prepared the way to the Father and became the foundation on which the glorious Church could be built. Jesus provided a dwelling place for God in His own life (Col. 2:9), and in so doing enabled others to also experience God's abiding presence in their own lives.

WEEK 2

# The Outer Court

## Opening Icebreaker

Copycats. A volunteer should follow the leader's movements.

## Bible Readings

- Exodus 30:17–21; 38:1–20
- Ephesians 5:25–27
- James 1:22–25

## Opening Our Eyes

### The outer court

The outer court consisted of an oblong linen fence hung between sixty posts and was approximately 46 metres long by 23 metres wide and nearly 3 metres high. There were twenty posts along each side and ten posts at each end. Each post rested on a brass socket and had a silver cap at the top. A silver bar slotted into each cap and connected adjoining posts forming a curtain rail. The use of silver is important. The silver came from the half-shekel tax; it did not form part of the freewill offerings. It was known as atonement money (Exod. 30:11–16). The silver levy was, like circumcision, an act of obedience; it did not of itself secure salvation. A linen fence hung from this rail to the ground like a wall. At the eastern end of the linen fence was an entrance made of an embroidered curtain often referred to as the gate (Exod. 27:16). Inside this area towards the far end was a large tent about 15 metres long, 4 metres wide and 4 metres high covered with various curtains and animal skins. This contained the Holy Place and the Holy of Holies.

In the symbolism of the antiquity the square symbolised the universe as the sphere of divine revelation. The Holy of Holies was apparently a perfect cube (see 1 Kings 6:19ff), representing the ideal of heavenly perfection, God's kingdom established in Israel; whilst the oblong shape of the structure as a whole conveyed the present incompleteness of that kingdom. The direction in which it was set up, towards the four ends of the earth, showed that the kingdom planted in Israel was intended to embrace the entire world. The architecture of the tabernacle was "a copy and a shadow of what is in heaven" (Heb. 8:5), which is revealed to John as the New Jerusalem "coming down out of heaven from God" (Rev. 21:2, 16).

Within the linen walls of the outer court there were two main items of furniture called the bronze altar and the bronze basin. Aaron and his sons were to wash upon entering the Tent of Meeting and upon approaching the altar, where they were to present an offering to the Lord by fire for their consecration. These furnishings symbolised cleansing and consecration.

**Bronze altar**

The altar was the place where sacrifices were made and then burnt, including those of consecration and dedication. The Hebrew word for altar is *mizbeach* and means "slaughter place". It stood immediately inside the tabernacle walls and signified that the only way to a holy God was through a sacrifice for sin and without that sacrifice no further progress was possible. It was not just that a sinner made a sacrifice, but that it was a representative death of the sinner in their offering. That offering had to be totally pure without blemish or sin (Lev. 1:2–4). It speaks of the sacrifice of Jesus who was the "Lamb of God who takes away the sin of the world" (John 1:29), a full, perfect and sufficient sacrifice that paid the price for sin once and for all.

**Bronze basin**

The basin was made from the mirrors of the Israelite women (Exod. 38:8) and was filled with water. As the priests looked into it they would have seen anything unclean and would then have washed themselves. For Christians, the Word now has the function that ceremonial washing once had for the priests. In Ephesians Paul speaks of Christ's making the Church holy, "cleansing her by the washing with water through the word" (5:26). Though Jesus pronounced the disciples "clean" as He washed their feet on the evening of the Last Supper, He also emphasised their ongoing need for cleansing (John 13:10). It is by hiding God's Word in our hearts and obeying it that we can cleanse our way (Psa. 119:9, 11).

## Discussion Starters

1. How are you encouraged by the symbolism of the tabernacle's design and construction?

2. What did the death of an animal signify?

3. With the image of the bronze basin in mind, what similar functions does the Word of God fulfil in the lives of Christians?

4. Although we have been made clean by the blood of Christ, why is self-examination in the light of God's truth so important?

5. What methods of reading the Bible have you found most effective and why?

**6.** How has God's Word revealed areas in your own life that have needed cleansing or changing?

**7.** When and how did you come to believe in Christ's death for your sins?

**8.** What favourite scriptures have you "hidden in your heart" and why?

**9.** How does the outer court combine the truth of God's judgement and mercy?

## Personal Application

There is only one way to the Father and that is through faith in the death of Jesus for our sins. There can be no true progress in the spiritual life until we come to believe and accept His sacrifice for us. Christians are not people who admire the teachings of Jesus or even try to follow them, but those who first believe in Christ's death to save them from punishment for their sins.

A mirror is there to prevent you shaming yourself. It only reflects the truth about you so you can put right what is wrong. We need to spend time looking into the mirror of God's Word and allow the Holy Spirit to show us our own faults and weaknesses. The truths of the Bible can also help wash away our selfish attitudes and wrong opinions, replacing them with true love, compassion and understanding. At the basin of the Bible we can be cleansed from impure contact with a fallen world (John 13:10). Reading and meditating on Scripture is part of the process of renewing our mind (Rom. 12:2), so our thought life becomes pure and holy (Phil. 4:8).

## Seeing Jesus in the Scriptures

Jesus is the ultimate sacrifice. He was completely pure without blemish or sin and totally consecrated to doing the will of God. Jesus was hung on a wooden cross where He was judged and punished instead of us. In John 15:22 Jesus spoke of the revealing nature of His words, and in John 13:1–10 and 15:3 He spoke of their cleansing power. Through faith in Him, following His teaching, we become like Him in love and sacrifice.

WEEK 3

# The Holy Place

## Opening Icebreaker

Blindfold some volunteers and ask them to write their name and the words "Praise the Lord for He is great" and draw an outline of Great Britain on a piece of paper. Show the group how well (or badly!) people have been able to perform without their sight.

## Bible Readings

- Exodus 25:25–40, 30:1–10, 34–38
- Leviticus 24:5–9

## Opening Our Eyes

The Holy Place was constructed by assembling wooden boards overlaid with gold to form three sides of a tent. Animal skins were laid over the top to form a roof and a curtain hung across the open entrance. Another curtain, the veil, hung inside the tent and separated the Holy Place from the Holy of Holies. There were three items of furniture inside the Holy Place:

### Gold lampstand

This was a seven-branched oil lamp which provided light in the otherwise dark interior of the Holy Place. Beside serving this practical purpose, the lampstand also had a symbolic significance, bearing as it did the holy light of God and so expressing Israel's relation to God. In Revelation 1:12, 20 and 2:5, similar symbolism is used, only the lampstands now represent the churches. The lampstand can also be seen as referring to Christ, the light of the world (John 8:12). Wrought of a single piece of gold it had a central stem and three branches on either side, shaped like almond flowers with buds and blossom. The description is reminiscent of John 15 where Jesus is the vine and we are the branches. He supplies strength and life to the whole Body. We are one with Him. His life is the light of men (John 1:4). In Zechariah 4:2–6, the lampstand also refers to the Holy Spirit, who is likened to oil burning from a seven-branched lamp. Just as it was important for the wicks to be trimmed in order to allow the oil to burn brightly, so the Lord sometimes seeks to trim or prune us in order that our light might shine more effectively.

### Gold table of showbread

The purpose of the table was to display and "show" twelve loaves of bread before the Lord for seven days, after which the priests could eat them, replacing the bread with another twelve loaves. The bread was made with fine flour and is seen to signify a pure life and heart examined and approved by God. There was a loaf for each of the twelve tribes of Israel, representing them before God both individually and as one nation. In this offering the tribes are together humbled before God – there is no difference, for all fall short of His glory. The loaves were sprinkled with incense to emphasise that they had been consecrated for holy use, for "an offering made to the Lord by fire", and once consecrated, are to be consumed by priests in the holy place (Lev. 24:5–9). The word for "showbread" is sometimes translated "bread of the Presence", indicating that the loaves, and so the people of Israel, are made holy, "acceptable" to the Lord, by being prepared and set apart in this way. For Christians, Jesus is now the "bread of life", broken for us, offered on our behalf, that we might know the friendship and fellowship of the Father (John 6:48–58).

**Gold altar of incense**

Incense speaks of prayer and praise (Rev. 5:8). This altar was for burning incense, symbolising our worship, by which we draw near to God (Psa. 141:1–2). It was positioned immediately in front of the thick curtaining of the veil, which separated the Holy Place from the Holy of Holies where God's presence dwelt among His people. As the place of prayer and intercession it reminds us of Jesus who is the mediator (1 Tim. 2:5), always interceding for us (Heb. 7:25) and sending His Spirit to help us in our weakness (Rom. 8:26–27). The first altar, for sacrifice, was made with wood and bronze, but this one was made with wood and gold, the most precious of all metals, drawing a sharp distinction between the court of the people and the sanctuary of the Lord.

## Discussion Starters

1. How does the symbolism of the lampstand encourage you to think of Jesus and the Holy Spirit?

2. What causes your light to be dimmed and how could your life be trimmed to shine more effectively?

3. Define purity of heart and holiness, "without which no man shall see the Lord".

4. The priests ate bread before God that had been examined by Him. How important is self-examination when taking communion?

5. With the image of the golden altar in mind, why do you think our prayers are important to God?

**6.** How does the Lord's Prayer combine both prayer and praise? How can this be a model for our own prayers?

**7.** Discuss the differences between prayer, praise and intercession? What are your personal experiences of each?

**8.** How do we balance the truths of the purity Christ gives that we cannot attain, with our personal responsibility to then live a pure life?

**9.** Why is it so important that Jesus is always praying for us?

**10.** What keys to deeper fellowship with God are revealed in the Holy Place?

## Personal Application

Both the outer court and the Holy Place emphasise the need for purity in our approach to God. In the outer court purity is based on what Jesus has done for us in His perfect sacrifice typified by the bronze altar, and provision of His Word typified by the bronze basin. In the Holy Place we see the importance of our continuing reliance on Christ and the Holy Spirit; although we are exhorted to put off sinful practices and put on a new life of holiness to the Lord (Eph. 4:17–31). Ultimately our sanctification is the Spirit's work. We are to enter God's presence with thanksgiving flowing from pure hearts of praise (Psa. 100:4; Phil. 4:4–7), and not just the words of our lips, which may not reflect a holy lifestyle (Matt. 15:7). As New Testament priests we are called to intercession for our world that others may come to know God (1 Tim. 2:1–4). Above all else, the Holy Place speaks of a friendship and fellowship that we can enjoy with our awesome God. Our priceless privilege is to feed by faith on Christ, the bread of life, because we are invited as special guests to sit down with Him at His table, and experience His wonderful companionship.

## Seeing Jesus in the Scriptures

Jesus is the light of the world, He is the bread of life, and He is the Great Intercessor.

WEEK 4

# The Holy of Holies

## Opening Icebreaker

Who's there? Blindfold some volunteers and then ask them to identify other members of the group by just feeling their noses. If that's too personal just feel their hands and fingers!

## Bible Readings

- Exodus 25:10–22; 26:31–33;
- Hebrews 9:2–5

## Opening Our Eyes

### The veil

The veil was a thick curtain hung across the tent and separated the Holy Place from the Holy of Holies. It was in the Holy of Holies that God actually dwelt. Although without natural light, it is filled with the brightness of the *shekinah*, the glory or light of God's presence. The veil was embroidered with cherubim, signifying that within the veil was the Holy of Holies. Cherubim also represent guardianship, as at the entrance to the Garden of Eden (Gen. 3:24). Once a year, on the Day of Atonement, the high priest would pull back the curtain to carry burning coals from the altar of incense into the Holy of Holies and sprinkle blood onto the mercy seat to atone for the sins of the people committed in ignorance (Lev. 16). Although He had made His dwelling among them, God was nevertheless apart from Israel; unapproachable, except through perpetual sacrifice; the problem of how a sinful people could stand in the presence of a holy God remained. Hebrews tells us that only when Christ entered the presence of God, by the blood of His own sacrifice, offered on our behalf, was the problem resolved and the way into the Holy of Holies opened for us (Heb. 9:8–14). This was symbolised by the tearing of the curtain in the Temple at the moment of Christ's death (Matt. 27:51; cf. Heb. 10:19–20).

### Ark of the covenant

This was an open wooden box or chest overlaid with gold and containing a pot of manna, Aaron's rod that budded and the commandments written on the tablets of stone (Heb. 9:4). That the ark contained the tablets given at Sinai underscores that the central purpose of God's making His dwelling among the people of Israel, is to set apart for Himself a holy nation. The law is holy; thus, in obedience to it, the worshipper becomes "like Him":

indeed Jesus' fulfilment of the law is how we know that His righteousness was divine. Although we are saved, like Israel delivered from slavery in Egypt, by grace, it is to the law, interpreted for us by Christ (Mark 12:28–34), that we must conform our obedience. The manna was a reminder of how God had sustained Israel in the wilderness and of God's provision for man's need. God had instructed Moses to keep a jar of the manna and have Aaron place it before the Lord in front of the stone tablets as a lasting testimony to His sufficiency (Exod. 16:32–34). This speaks of Jesus, the provision of God to meet man's need. Finally, Aaron's budded staff was kept as a sign to the rebellious tribes that the Levitical priesthood had been chosen and approved by God Himself (Num. 17). Aaron's staff had blossomed into new life – it held forth the promise of God's mercy in face of Israel's disobedience.

**Mercy seat**

This formed a lid for the open ark and covered its contents. The commandments revealed our sin, declared our guilt and pronounced our punishment. God graciously covered the law with His mercy. The lid was sprinkled once a year with the blood of the atoning sacrifice by the high priest, to obtain God's mercy: for Christians, Christ's blood "covers" our sin and his mercy is on those who put their trust in him. With Paul in Romans 4:7–8 we may sing with the psalmist:

*Blessed are they*
*whose transgressions are forgiven,*
*Whose sins are covered.*
*Blessed is the man*
*whose sin the Lord will never count against him.*

## Discussion Starters

1. Why was the veil necessary and what did it signify?

2. What does the fact that the ark contained the tablets of the law tell us about God's purposes for Israel?

3. How does the law lead us to Christ? (Gal. 3:15–25)

4. Why did the commandments have to be covered over?

5. What was the purpose of including the manna among the holy things to be placed in the ark?

**6.** In what ways did the contents of the ark, in particular Aaron's staff represent both judgement and mercy?

**7.** Do you feel chosen by God? What has He chosen you for?

**8.** Why will God never judge you for your sins but always show mercy?

## Personal Application

Perhaps the most important application is found in Hebrews 4:16, which encourages us to approach the throne of grace with confidence to receive mercy and grace in time of need. Christ, our great High Priest, has made a way for us to enter the very throne room of God our Father. God welcomes us into His presence with open arms and looks on our failings and sins with mercy and forgiveness because of the sprinkled blood of His Son. We are not to come before Him in cringing fear but we have a legal right and open invitation to approach His throne. Perhaps like a prince approaching his father, the king; with respect and honour, but above all love and a feeling that the king desires us to be with him.

Many people struggle with rejection, but God has specifically chosen you to receive His life, bear His beauty and produce His fruit through your relationship with Him. As you receive nourishment from the Word and Spirit of God you will grow up into Christ, bearing the fragrance of His love and life to others.

## Seeing Jesus in the Scriptures

Jesus is represented in the contents of the ark because He is the true manna from heaven (John 6:51), the fruitful Branch (Isa. 4:2, 11:1) and the Word of God (John 1:1). His body is also the veil rent asunder, opening the way for us to the Holy of Holies, the very presence of God (Heb. 10:19–22) and an atoning sacrifice for us, through faith (Rom. 3:25). The letter to the Hebrews says that it is His blood that is sprinkled over us, cleansing our hearts and consciences of their sin. Jesus, like Aaron, was rejected by men but chosen and approved by God Himself as our great High Priest.

WEEK 5

# The Priesthood

## Opening Icebreaker

Ask the group to list negative images of religious leaders portrayed in the media, such as in TV comedies, books, films and press reports. Then ask them to list what they think are the qualities that a religious leader should display.

## Bible Readings

- Exodus 28 & 29
- Leviticus 10:1–3
- Numbers 16:42–49

## Opening Our Eyes

The ordination of the priesthood was a vital part in the establishment of the tabernacle. Priests were mediators between God and man, and without them there would have been no acceptable sacrifices and God would not have made Himself present among the people. We can identify several important aspects in the inauguration of the priesthood.

The priests were specifically **chosen** by God. It was His idea and He chose those who He wanted to serve as priests. This privilege and responsibility fell to Aaron and his sons, Nadab, Abihu, Eleazar and Ithmar. They did not earn or pay for this honour, but the priesthood was graciously bestowed upon them by God Himself. It later caused controversy and jealousy when Korah tried to usurp the position for himself (Num. 16). His rebellion led to the miracle when a rod for each tribe was placed before God and it was Aaron's staff that sprouted buds, blossom and fruit (Num. 17), indicating that the tribe of Levi had been chosen. Although all the Levites were to serve in the tabernacle, only the descendants of Aaron could actually be priests, ministering at the altar and in the tent.

The priests were then **cleansed** by washing in water (Exod. 29:4). This ritual symbolised the need for purity before the Lord; later it was prescribed as necessary whenever the priests entered the Tent of Meeting or approached the altar for ministry (Exod. 30:17–21). It is similar in effect to that referred to in Psalm 119:9–11; John 13:10, 15:3 and Ephesians 5:25–26, effected by the water of the Word of God purifying our attitudes and daily walk in a fallen world.

The priests were **clothed** in special garments. The high priest wore a fine linen robe covered by a blue tunic, colourful waistcoat and jewelled breastplate. Aaron wore on his head a linen turban, on which was a gold plate inscribed with the words, "Holy To The Lord". The hem of his tunic was decorated with bells and pomegranates signifying life and fruitfulness.

The priests were **consecrated**, following the sin and burnt offerings, by being set apart and made holy by the blood of a sacrificial animal put on their ears, thumbs and toes. This symbolised a cleansing and continuing purity of their mind, what they did and where they went. They were also sprinkled with the special anointing oil signifying the power and ministry of the Holy Spirit in their lives.

Finally, the priests were **commissioned** for service to God and a life of intimacy with Him. They would eat their share of the ordination sacrifice, and a loaf of the showbread from the table as a sign of their privilege as priests. Their role was to act as mediator between God and the Israelites. The priests represented God to the people and they represented the people before God. It was the intercession of Aaron that halted the plague destroying the Israelites when they deserved God's judgement. The priests offered sacrifices brought by the people for expiation of their sins. On the annual Day of Atonement, Aaron offered sacrificial blood to atone for sins committed in ignorance and so reconcile God and His chosen nation. The priests were also custodians of God's Word and responsible for the implementation of its principles (Lev. 10:11; Deut. 31:9–13); thus when Nadab and Abihu went beyond the prescription of the law, exceeding their responsibilities and offering "unauthorized fire" before the Lord, they had to be put to death (Lev. 10:1–5).

## Discussion Starters

1. What was the purpose of the priesthood and why was it necessary?

2. What were the requirements of being a priest in the tabernacle?

3. What was the significance of the cleansing and how do we as New Testament believers purify ourselves before the Lord?

4. What did the priests' special clothing and consecration signify?

5. Why do you think it was important that they were commissioned?

**6.** How can we be holy in a fallen world?

**7.** Nadab and Abihu's punishment impresses on us the importance of taking God's Word seriously. What does it mean for us to be obedient in our discipleship?

**8.** How are we cleansed by both water and blood?

**9.** What qualities does a mediator need in order to bring people together?

## Personal Application

According to 1 Peter 2:5–9 and Revelation 1:4–6 all New Testament believers are classified as priests to serve God. We have been **chosen** (Eph. 1:4, 11; 1 Pet. 2:9), **cleansed** (Titus 3:3–7; Heb. 10:22; 1 John 1:9), **clothed** (Gal. 3:27), **consecrated** (Acts 1:8; 1 Cor. 6:11) and **commissioned** (Matt. 28:18–20). Our first responsibility is to offer our very selves as living sacrifices, holy and pleasing to God (Rom. 12:1). We are called to eat with Him at His table as a symbol of our intimate friendship (Rev. 3:20). We have also been entrusted with God's Word of the Good News of Jesus Christ, with the ministry of reconciliation whereby we bring together the lost and the Good Shepherd who searches for His sheep (2 Cor. 5:17–20).

As priests we must pursue a life of personal holiness, purifying "ourselves from everything that contaminates body and spirit, perfecting holiness out of reverence for God" (2 Cor. 7:1). Then we fulfil our chosen calling by producing spiritual fruit of love, joy, peace, patience, kindness, goodness, faithfulness, gentleness and self-control (John 15:16; Gal. 5:22–23).

## Seeing Jesus in the Scriptures

Jesus is the great High Priest (Heb. 4:14) and the only true mediator between God and man (1 Tim. 2:5). He permanently intercedes for us before the Father (Heb. 7:24–25). The high priest bore the names of the tribes of Israel on his shoulders and heart (Exod. 28:12, 15–21, 29) – the place of strength and the seat of love. Jesus bears your name before the throne of God so you may receive the Father's almighty strength and overwhelming love.

WEEK 6

# The Sacrificial System

## Opening Icebreaker - Penalties

If you were a judge, what penalties would you impose on a car thief, embezzler, child molester, drunk driver, drug dealer and murderer? If a husband forgets his wedding anniversary what should he do?

## Bible Readings

- Leviticus 1:1–9; 2:1–3; 3:1–5; 4:27–31; 5:1–6, 14–19; 16:1–34

## Opening Our Eyes

The key to God dwelling among His people and our understanding of the tabernacle is the sacrificial system. It is also the key to fully understanding the death of Jesus and the completeness of our salvation. There can be no approach of sinful man to a holy God without sacrifice (Heb. 9:22). God is too pure for sin to exist in His presence (Hab. 1:13) and so our sins separate us from God (Isa. 59:2). We are no longer *at one* with Him. The stain and guilt of sin can only be cleansed and removed by the death of the sinner (Rom. 6:23). However, God will accept a perfect substitute in place of the sinner, who can then walk free, forgiven of sin and now *at one* with God (Lev. 17:11). When sacrifices were made, people would lay their hands on an innocent animal. This symbolised a transfer of sin and life from the person to the sacrifice, and a transfer of purity and life from the blameless animal to the person making the offering. There were many different offerings including the Passover and those for "uncleanness" such as leprosy and bodily discharges. We will only consider the five main sacrifices plus the Day of Atonement. The first three were "sweet savour" offerings producing an "aroma pleasing to the Lord" because they were voluntary or freewill offerings.

The **burnt offering** was one of devotion or worship. It was typical of the offerings in that the animal had to be perfect. This was not just on the outside but, because it was skinned and cut into pieces, inner defects would also have been revealed. God later condemned His people for using imperfect sacrifices (Mal. 1:6–14). The entire flesh of the burnt offering was consumed on the altar, signifying the complete dedication of the individual or of the nation to God.

The **meal offering** consisted of grain, usually crushed in the form of fine flour, which could be baked into cakes.

The fine flour signified purity and holiness and was a testimony and appreciation of God's daily provision. It could not contain any yeast or honey because the processes by which these were produced made them unsuitable for use at the altar. Instead it was sprinkled with salt, perhaps as a sign of the permanence and incorruptibility of God's covenant with His people. The offering of firstfruits was crushed heads of new grain, reminding us of John 12:24, where Jesus is the ear of wheat crushed to death in the ground so He could produce many seeds.

The **peace offering** was one of thanksgiving to God and celebrated fellowship with Him. It was actually the fifth offering, as peace with God could only come after the sin and trespass offerings had been made. The peace offering is listed at this point because it is the third of the voluntary offerings.

The **sin offering** atones for sins committed either intentionally or unintentionally against God or neighbour.

The **trespass** or **guilt offering** significantly includes repayment for the damage caused by sin in the form of injury or loss of property. In Isaiah 53:10 the self-surrender of God's servant is seen as a trespass offering. Christ atones and makes reparation for our sin; He gives to God what we have withheld from Him.

The **Day of Atonement** was a special annual event when sacrifices were offered for all those sins that remained un-atoned for. After making atonement for the Holy of Holies, the Tent of Meeting and the altar, a "scapegoat" was chosen to carry the community's sins away into the desert, and there to die.

## Discussion Starters

1. Why was it that only blood could purge sin?

2. Why did the sacrifice have to be perfect?

3. What did the laying on of hands signify?

4. Why does sin carry a penalty? Why does God just not overlook sin because He loves us?

5. What could not be used in sacrifices and why? What had to be used?

**6.** What is the significance of the fact that the peace offerings followed the sin and guilt offerings?

**7.** Why are unintentional sins still classed as sins?

**8.** Can you recall the time when you confessed and were cleansed of sin?

**9.** Are all sins equally bad?

**10.** Have you been guilty of offering God imperfect sacrifices?

## Personal Application

As unbelievers our sins separated us from God. It was only through the death of Jesus that we are reconciled to Him. There was nothing we could do to pay or cancel the debt of our sins, but Christ paid it all and became the scapegoat for all our wrongdoings (Eph. 2:1–9). It can be all too easy to forget or neglect the once for all time sacrifice of Jesus on our behalf, especially if we have been Christians for several years. In view of God's astonishing mercy, let us offer ourselves, freely and gladly, as living sacrifices to God. Let this be our spiritual act of worship.

## Seeing Jesus in the Scriptures

Christ is the voluntary burnt offering, in total submission to God's will. He is the meal offering in His sinless service and, with the blood of the cross, He is also a peace offering for us, restoring us to fellowship with God. The sin offering symbolises Christ as our guilt-bearer and the trespass offering typifies His payment for the damage caused by our sinful acts. He is the atoning sacrifice who carries away the burden of our sin to reconcile us to God.

WEEK 7

# Jesus and the Tabernacle

## Opening Icebreaker

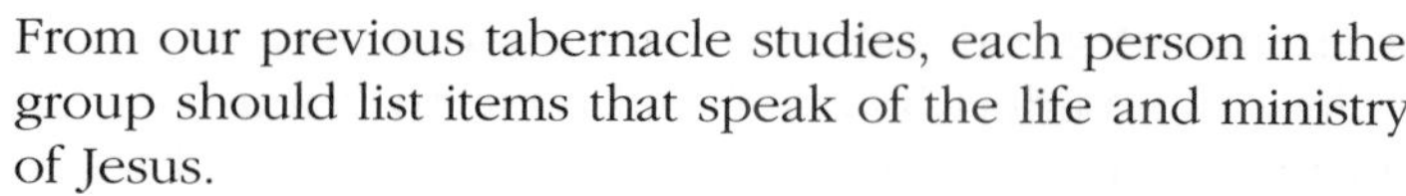

From our previous tabernacle studies, each person in the group should list items that speak of the life and ministry of Jesus.

## Bible Readings

- Hebrews 2:10–18; 4:14–15; 9:1–10:22; 13:15

## Opening Our Eyes

The construction of the tabernacle, the inauguration of the priesthood and the establishment of the sacrificial system was considered so important by God that He even authored a book in the New Testament to explain its significance and applicability to Jesus Christ and those who believe in Him. The way to God in the tabernacle was through sacrifice at the bronze altar, washing in the bronze basin, eating the showbread illuminated by the candlestick, offering incense at the golden altar and then, once a year, sprinkling the blood of atonement on the mercy seat. The way to God now is to accept the sacrifice of Jesus, wash and feed on the Word of God illuminated by the Holy Spirit, offer ourselves as "living sacrifices" and proclaim the blood of Christ as we boldly draw near to our heavenly Father.

The high priest had to be a true man in order that he could fully represent man before God. Jesus became fully human in order that He could be the great High Priest who was subject to all our frailties, yet without sin. The blood of bulls and goats could only "cover" human sin but not actually remove it. That is why it was necessary for an annual sacrifice on the Day of Atonement. Only the sacrifice of a perfect human could perfectly remove human sin, but no perfect human ever existed, until Jesus. God made Him fully human so that in His sinless life and innocent death, human sin could be totally cleansed forever! No seating was provided in the tabernacle because the priest's work was never done. He was continually offering sacrifices for sin. When Jesus offered His own blood to God He sat down at the Father's right hand because His offering meant that the sacrificial system was finished! The debt created by sin was not just "covered over", but totally cancelled (John 19:30; Col. 2:13–14). The curtain of the veil had always separated man from God in the Holy of Holies, but in Christ the veil is removed so that we have open and permanent access to the Father (Matt. 27:51; Heb. 10:19–22). To deny that we can personally draw near to God because of our sinfulness is to deny the work of Jesus on the cross, which has removed all our guilt and shame. We are not just ceremonially and outwardly cleansed, but faith in Christ's blood actually purges our consciences of guilt (Heb. 9:14). In tabernacle sacrifices, sin was transferred from the sinner to the innocent animal. We see this principle at work in Isaiah 53 and especially 2 Corinthians 5:21: "For God took the sinless Christ and poured into him our sins. Then, in exchange, he poured God's goodness into us!" (TLB). One chorus says, "When God looks at me, He sees not what I used to be, but He sees Jesus." Christ has become our righteousness, holiness and redemption (1 Cor. 1:30). We have not just been cleansed, however, we have also been made priests ourselves (1 Pet. 2:9; Rev. 1:5–6).

In His death Jesus not only took upon Himself the role of High Priest but He was also the consummation of all of the sacrifices in His one offering on the cross. The only role that remains for us in the sacrificial system is to offer the sacrifice of praise for what God has already done for us in the death of Jesus.

## Discussion Starters

1. Why was it necessary for Jesus to be fully human?

2. Why were animal sacrifices repeated every year?

3. How did Jesus fulfil the role of High Priest?

4. Why is Jesus' sacrifice better than animals?

5. How do we "lay hands" on Jesus and transfer our sin?

**6.** Would you say that you had a guilty conscience or a clean conscience?

**7.** What spiritual sacrifices can we still make?

**8.** How did Jesus fulfil the various sacrifices?

**9.** Do you feel God hears you when you pray?

**10.** What is the path to an intimate relationship with God?

## Personal Application

Jesus is the only way to God (John 14:6) and only by His Name can we be saved (Acts 4:12). God uses Christ's blood and our faith as a means of saving us from His judgement (Rom. 3:25). Simply knowing the lessons of the tabernacle is insufficient to save us. Salvation is only experienced when there is a personal choice to accept the death of Jesus as the atoning sacrifice for our sins. We must deliberately "lay our hands" on Jesus as the Lamb of God, and by faith transfer the guilt of our sins to receive the righteousness of Christ. Once that transaction has been made we can rejoice that we are made acceptable to God and can come to our heavenly Father as His special child.

## Seeing Jesus in the Scriptures

| | |
|---|---|
| **Jesus is the Offerer** | Christ in His person as a man |
| **Jesus is the Priest** | Christ in His office as mediator |
| **Jesus is the Offering** | Christ in His work as substitute |

# Leader's Notes

## Week 1: Preparing to Build

### Icebreaker

Occupations mimed could be as diverse, for example, as a dentist, bricklayer etc. The point is that everybody has a role in life and contributes in some way to their community.

### Bible Readings

There is probably too much to be read in the group meeting so carefully select appropriate verses. You may also wish to refer to the parable of the talents (Matt. 25:14–29; Luke 19:11–26). The readings are meant to convey the excitement of being involved in the work of God and the fact that everyone has an important part to play.

### Aim of the Session

An understanding that little of consequence is achieved without preparation. A doctor studies for years before qualifying. A building requires the clearing of land and the digging of deep foundations before it can be constructed. The development of people and projects requires vision, plans, enthusiasm and sheer hard work. The Church is not like a football match where 11 people do the running around while 50,000 spectate or even walk out if things are going badly. The Church is a living organism and we all have a part to play depending on our abilities and circumstances. Our personal goal should be to serve Christ's Body by discovering our gifts, developing them as far as possible and then using them to build up the Church and reach out to others. Above all else we need a sense of God's majesty and the holiness of the calling that He places on us, as our motivation and strength. But first and foremost we need to remember that God comes to us as a friend to make His dwelling among us. God's love for us is our incentive to work with Him; within that love we may experience the fulfilment of being a useful and fully functioning member of Christ's Body, contributing in some small way to His eternal purposes.

In this session we need to focus on encouragement and possibilities rather than condemnation of previous lack of involvement. We also should be sensitive to individual circumstances where people are already stressed because of personal demands such as physical frailty, finance, family and job pressures. Even Israelite soldiers were excused from army service for the first year of marriage (Deut. 24:5)!

---

## **Week 2:** The Outer Court

### Icebreaker

You will need two small plates, one for you and one for a volunteer. Prior to the meeting, smear the underneath of one plate with dirt, e.g. smoke from a lighted match. Sit inches apart facing the volunteer who should copy your actions all the time only looking at you. Holding the untreated plate on the palm and fingers of one hand use the other hand to rub the surface of the plate and then gently rub your face. Rub the underneath of the plate and rub your face. Swap hands and repeat the movements. If your volunteer has followed your movements exactly he or she should now have a dirty face. After looking in a mirror let him or her wash away the marks using tissues and a small bowl of water. The point is that we do not know we are not clean until we look in a mirror and then we need water to wash away the uncleanness. This speaks of the bronze basin in the outer court. Be careful your volunteer does not ruin their best clothes!

**Visual Display**

Whenever we communicate we should try to remember and utilise the principle that 80 per cent of information is gathered through our eyes rather than our ears. It can be great fun and highly instructive if you or the group actually make a model of the tabernacle. This should be as simple as possible and not detract from the study itself.

The outer court could be made from four pieces of narrow card covered with cloth to form an oblong twice as long as it is wide. The bronze altar can be made from a matchbox covered in paper and the basin from a small eggcup, both painted a bronze colour or covered in bronze-coloured paper. The tent requires three pieces of card covered in gold paper. When they are joined together, coloured material can be suspended from thin wires at the entrance and in the middle to separate the Holy Place from the Holy of Holies. Over the top lay several different pieces of material to form a removable roof. The table of showbread and altar of incense can be made from more matchboxes but this time covered in gold paper. The seven-branched candlestick could be made from pipe cleaners or modelling clay and again covered in gold paper. An open matchbox can be the ark, using a cover to make a lid – the mercy seat – both covered in gold paper. Draw and cut out two cherubim in gold paper and attach them to the lid. There you have it, your very own tabernacle!

Visual display is a vital part of understanding the tabernacle so even if you cannot make a model try at least to find some relevant pictures in Bible handbooks.

### Aim of the Session

To achieve an understanding of the physical layout of the tabernacle and the spiritual truths revealed in the construction of the outer court, the bronze altar and basin. In particular, to fully appreciate the necessity of faith in the sacrificial death of Jesus, and the importance of reading God's Word if we are to draw close to Him and enjoy His presence.

---

## **Week 3:** The Holy Place

### Icebreaker

The point of this exercise is that without light we perform very badly and make mistakes. We need the light of God's Word and His Spirit to see clearly in order to live a holy and fruitful life and experience the joy of His presence. This speaks of the Holy Place, and in particular the showbread and the golden candlestick.

### Aim of the Session

To achieve an understanding of the physical layout of the Holy Place and the spiritual truths revealed in the construction of the lampstand, table of showbread and altar of incense. The Holy Place is just that – a place which is holy. The New Testament explains that we can only be made holy by faith in the shed blood of Christ to cleanse us from sin, but it balances this truth with our personal responsibility to live a holy life. This is not a contradiction but complementary teachings. Sanctification and holiness are both a position and a process. We have been made holy, we are being made holy and we will be made holy. Ephesians 4:17–32 is a prime example of this requirement to live a holy lifestyle. The path to intimacy with God firstly requires that we are purified by Christ's sacrifice for us, typified by the bronze altar, and then we purify ourselves by Christ's life and Spirit flowing through us, typified by the Holy Place.

The bronze altar was situated in the outer court in the open air, natural light and public gaze of others. The Holy Place was within the tent, a private place lit only by the lampstand. Our initial personal commitment to Christ is often a public event in the presence of others who lead us to faith. Our ongoing relationship with God ultimately only deepens through personal and private devotional times feeding on God's Word illuminated by His Spirit. We present ourselves to God for Him to examine and correct us, but we also spend time in private worship, personal prayer and intercession for the needs of others.

The Holy Place is not an experience to be feared but one to be enjoyed as we draw closer to the Lord and the joy of His presence. The letter to the Hebrews says that we are to approach God with confidence, "with a sincere heart in full assurance of faith" (Heb. 10:19–22). The Holy Place is a place of friendship and fellowship where our hearts are fed with His comfort, strength and love. Our spirits burn with passion as we pour out our praises and prayers at the altar of incense, and our understanding of Him is enlarged as He reveals and illuminates our minds to more of the glories of His person and the wonders of His ways.

There is so much we cannot understand about God by our natural senses, but in the Holy Place the Spirit of God can reveal the deep and otherwise unsearchable riches of God and what He has accomplished in us who believe in Christ (1 Cor. 2; Eph. 1:15–23; 3:14–21). This is not an earthly wisdom based on intelligence or education but a direct revelation given to those who take the time to draw aside and offer themselves to Him.

## **Week 4:** The Holy of Holies

### Icebreaker

The aim of this icebreaker is to show how difficult it is to identify someone unless we can see them. While similar to the last icebreaker this time its emphasis is not upon what we do or comprehend but upon our relationships with others. It is difficult to truly know another person unless we can see them clearly or understand their thoughts and actions. In the Old Testament God dwelt behind a veil. He did reveal Himself to people such as Moses and David but even then it was a partial and not a clear image. This was partly due to man's sin obscuring a true picture of God and partly for man's own protection because of his inability to see the glorious holiness of God and live. The Israelites could not even bear to look at Moses when he had been in God's presence because of reflected glory. We read in 2 Corinthians 3:7–18 that in Christ the veil is removed so we can clearly see and understand the glory of God and be changed into His likeness.

### Aim of the Session

To achieve an understanding of the physical layout of the Holy of Holies and the spiritual truths revealed in the veil, ark and mercy seat. There are two particularly valuable lessons that can be learnt.

The first is the character and effect of God's laws. Although they are pure and righteous, their effect is to condemn us because their demand on us is infinite. It is through the law that we become conscious of sin (Rom. 3:20). The law is powerless to deliver us from its own judgement, because none of us can perfectly fulfil its requirements (Gal. 2:16). It is therefore by grace that we are saved, through faith (Eph. 2:8). The ark not only contained the commandments on the stone tablets but, according to Deuteronomy 31:26, the whole Book of the Law was placed alongside it to serve as a witness against the Israelites. Even if we keep the whole law yet stumble at just one point we are guilty of breaking all of it (James 2:10). We are lawbreakers if we drop litter or commit murder. The consequences of the two acts are obviously different but both are prohibited by law. There are even sins of omission when we fail to do the good things we know we should (James 4:17). That is why all have sinned and fall short of God's standard (Rom. 3:23). We therefore need to look in a different direction for salvation from the law's judgements and so the law becomes a teacher that directs us from itself to Christ who did fulfil its demands and died in our place (Rom. 3:21–22; Gal. 3:10–25). Salvation, then, is not a product of keeping the law, which we are unable to do, but of faith in Christ. The stone tablets in the ark represent the unchanging laws of God, which would condemn us to death. The mercy seat with its sprinkled blood covered the law so that Israel would not be condemned, but Christ's own blood alone could make full atonement, enabling us to recover a proper understanding of the law (Rom. 10:2–4).

The second lesson is similar, in that even those who enthusiastically read, research and study the Scriptures can never truly understand and appreciate them apart from a real relationship with Jesus Christ. This is the message of the icebreaker and highlighted in 2 Corinthians 3:14–15. The point is that when we know an author personally, his or her writings come alive. When we know Jesus Christ, His Spirit will expand our finite minds to understand infinite and eternal truths so, just like the disciples on the road to Emmaus, our hearts will burn within us as He opens the Scriptures to us.

## **Week 5:** The Priesthood

### Icebreaker

The discussion is aimed to highlight the often vast gap between the perception of religious leaders in our culture and God's own perception and requirements of His priests. Ultimately we are all priests and should therefore aim for the highest standards of behaviour if we are to faithfully represent a holy God on earth.

### Aim of the Session

To achieve an understanding of the role of priests in the tabernacle and the necessity of personal holiness. We can then apply the learnt spiritual truths to ourselves as New Testament priests. The references in Exodus chapters 28 and 29 are probably too long to be read in full at a group meeting and you may therefore need to select appropriate verses. You may like to spread this study over two weeks because of the quantity and depth of teaching. It would be helpful if you could find a picture or diagram of the high priest for people to look at. In my own group I actually prepared various materials and dressed one of the members as Aaron, but without the precious jewels! The visual impact can be very beneficial in developing knowledge and understanding. One of the main lessons is that as New Testament priests we no longer need an intermediary but can personally approach God's throne (Heb. 4:16). It is a point previously considered when we looked at the Holy of Holies but bears repetition because it is one of the key teachings of this whole series. This does not mean we should all be church leaders (1 Cor. 12:27–30; Eph. 4:11), but it does mean we can all have a personal relationship with God.

It may be particularly helpful to focus on the personal application; to fully appreciate how the high priest bore the names of the tribes of Israel on his shoulders and heart before God. You could then compare this with Jesus and references such as Matthew 11:28–30 and John 15:13. This might provide an opportunity for people with specific burdens to share and receive prayer to receive God's strength, comfort and love.

The priests were called to high standards of personal holiness. We have already seen some of the requirements, but other passages such as Leviticus chapter 21 contain lists of regulations to ensure the purity of their lives. The story of the deaths of Nadab and Abihu can appear confusing, because if God had ordained them to the priesthood why would He then kill them for offering sacrifices? Their actions emphasise the need for purity because they appear to show gross disobedience and lack of respect for a holy God. Their offering was "contrary to God's command" and they used "unauthorised fire" (Lev. 10:1). Offerings made by fire should have used burning coals from the altar but they seem to have used their own man-made fire. Compare this story with Leviticus 16:12 and Numbers 16:46, where Aaron took fire from the altar and then put on incense. It was God's own fire that had started the fire on the altar (Lev. 9:24) and to use fire from any other source was an insult to Him. They could not approach God without the fire of sacrifice, and we cannot approach God save on the basis of the sacrifice of Jesus. Some commentators, because of the proximity of God's command in Leviticus 10:9, also believe Nadab and Abihu were drunk. Interestingly, the stories of both the "church in the wilderness" (Acts 7:38, AV) and the Early Church begin with God executing people whose offerings were marred by personal sin (Acts 5:1–11).

As New Testament priests we are similarly called to lives of personal holiness (2 Cor. 7:1; Eph. 4:17–32). Our righteousness comes from Christ Himself but we are then called to wear the "fine linen" of the "righteous acts of the saints" (Rev. 19:8). Our holiness is given by God to be lived out in our daily lives, in order to faithfully represent a holy God to a fallen world.

---

## **Week 6:** The Sacrificial System

### Icebreaker

The aim of the icebreaker is to encourage people to think about offences and how we should deal with the people who commit them. Is it right to simply overlook wrongdoing, or should we impose penalties, and what form should they take? Human experience shows that there is no true reconciliation without apology and some kind of restitution or sacrifice, even for the forgetful husband!

### Aim of the Session

To achieve an understanding of the five main sacrifices and what they typified. In particular, to understand the seriousness and consequences of sin from God's perspective. We may think of some sins as relatively minor but the truth is that all sin separates us from God and brings us under the judgement of death. The true gravity of sin can only be gauged in the revelation that Christ was called upon to die for all sins, even those we might consider as insignificant.

This session deals with the doctrine of substitutionary atonement whereby an innocent substitute can bear the punishment of death instead of the sinner, so reconciling him or her to God. This can be a difficult principle for people to accept because human nature wants to resolve its own problems and is too proud to accept help. However, all our righteousness is as filthy rags (Isa. 64:6) and we cannot pay the price of our own salvation. In modern times, there may also be a reluctance to accept the necessity of a blood sacrifice. However, God's requirements are unchanging, because it is only through the shedding of blood and taking of a life that sin can be punished and purged (Lev. 17:11; Heb. 9:22).

We see once again the requirements for purity in the offerings. There could be no yeast or honey, and the animals had to be pure not just on the outside, but on the inside as well. They were skinned and cut into pieces so any inward blemish would have been readily visible. We must always remember that God looks on the inside, which is why He chose David (1 Sam. 16:1–13) but killed Ananias and Sapphira (Acts 5:1–10).

Note that there were different sacrifices required for the same sin depending on the ability and responsibility of the person. For example, the sin of a priest required the same sacrifice as the sin of a nation (Lev. 4:3; 13–14). Wealthy people brought a lamb but if you could not afford it, two birds would suffice. God therefore made it possible for all people to be included and cleansed from sin regardless of wealth or privilege. He also emphasised the serious consequences of the sins of those in positions of authority and influence.

The annual Day of Atonement was a very special sacrifice that foreshadowed the wonderful day when our great High Priest, Jesus Christ, would offer Himself as the once and for all time atonement for the sins of the world. On that day the high priest would lay aside his glorious costume and enter the Holy of Holies clothed only in simple linen garments to present the blood of animals. Christ laid aside His heavenly glory and clothed Himself with the simple robe of human flesh to present His own atoning blood.

## **Week 7:** Jesus and the Tabernacle

### Icebreaker

The purpose of this exercise is as a memory jogger. By asking individuals to write lists it prevents those with the best memories and loudest voices from dominating the response!

### Aim of the Session

The aim of this session is to understand how perfectly Jesus fulfilled the Old Testament types of tabernacle, high priest and sacrifices. The key word to unlock the book of Hebrews is "better". Jesus did not just fulfil the types, He improved upon them! He was a better priest, offering better sacrifices, making a better covenant and providing a better forgiveness. For example, Aaron sinned, Jesus was sinless. Animal blood only "covered" sin, Jesus removed it. The sinner was outwardly cleansed but still had a guilty conscience, now even our conscience is cleansed. Only the high priest could approach God, and that only once a year, now we can approach God at any time.

The result of Jesus' sacrifice is that God now regards us as perfectly pure and holy in His sight and therefore we can draw near to Him in a relationship of deepest intimacy.

Jesus is the centre and culmination of all our studies on the tabernacle. Its construction, furniture, priesthood and sacrifices all speak prophetically of Him. As we conclude we need to remind ourselves that mere knowledge might only tickle our intellect and "puff us up". Scripture calls us to implement what we have learnt, otherwise, like the person looking in the mirror of James 1:22–25, we might end up deceiving ourselves.

Our first practical conclusion then is that people can only be cleansed from sin by confession and by placing their trust in Christ's sacrifice (1 John 1:9). Secondly, we are called to live as a holy priesthood, declaring the praises of the One who called us out of darkness into His wonderful light (1 Pet. 2:9). Finally, we are to develop an ever-deepening intimacy with our Heavenly Father, because the way to Him is now eternally opened to those who have become children of God (John 1:12).

In the words of the book of Hebrews: *"Therefore, brothers, since we have confidence to enter the Most Holy Place by the blood of Jesus, by a new and living way opened for us through the curtain, that is, his body, and since we have a great priest over the house of God, let us draw near to God with a sincere heart in full assurance of faith, having our hearts sprinkled to cleanse us from a guilty conscience and having our bodies washed with pure water"* (Heb. 10:19–22).

## Symbolism of the Offerings

| OFFERING | PURPOSE | TYPE |
|---|---|---|
| BURNT OFFERING | Worship | Voluntary |
| MEAL OFFERING | Purity & holiness | Voluntary |
| PEACE OFFERING | Thanksgiving & fellowship | Voluntary |
| SIN OFFERING | Deliverance from sin's power | Required for cleansing |
| TRESPASS OFFERING | Pardon of debts for sinful acts | Required for restitution & restoration |

| JESUS | PERSONAL APPLICATION |
|---|---|
| Devotion to God's will even unto death<br>Luke 22:42–44; Heb. 10:5–9 | Consecration of self<br>Rom. 12:1 |
| Sinless life<br>Finished work<br>Heb. 4:14–15<br>John 17:4; 19:30 | Consecration of gifts<br>purity of life & service<br>Rom. 12:2–8; Col. 3:1–17;<br>1 Cor. 5:8 |
| Reconciliation of God and man to intimacy<br>Rom. 5:1; 1 John 1:1–3 | Praise, fellowship and communion with God<br>Jonah 2:9; 1 Cor. 1:9<br>Heb. 13:15; 1 Pet. 2:9 |
| Atonement of man to God<br>Rom. 3:25; 1 John 2:2 | Confession & cleansing of sin<br>1 John 1:9 |
| Expiation and pardon of sins<br>Col. 2:13–14; 1 John 3:5 | Purifying the conscience and removal of guilt<br>2 Cor. 1:12; Heb. 9:14; 10:22 |

# Symbolism of the Tabernacle

| ITEM | PURPOSE | "TYPE" |
|---|---|---|
| **Gateway** | Way in to outer court | Way to know God |
| **Brass Altar** | Sacrifice | Sin offering |
| **Brass Basin** | Washing and cleansing | Word of God |
| **Door** | Door to Holy Place | Door to friendship with God |
| **Lampstand** | Light | Holy Spirit |
| **Table of Showbread** | Display bread | Communion |
| **Altar of Incense** | Burn incense | Intercession, praise |
| **Veil** | Entrance to Holy of Holies | Intimacy with God |
| **Ark of the Covenant** | Contain commandments<br>Contain manna<br>Contain Aaron's rod | God's laws<br>God's provision<br>God's choice and fru |
| **Mercy Seat** | Throne of God of Grace | Mercy |

| JESUS | PERSONAL APPLICATION |
|---|---|
| Way, John 14:6 | Come to God through Jesus |
| Lamb of God, John 1:29 | Cleansing by blood, 1 John 1:9 |
| Word of God, John 1:1 | Cleansing by Word, John 15:3 |
| Door, John 10:9 | Know God's Shepherd love, John 10 |
| Light of the World, John 8:12 | Our light to shine, Matt. 5:14–16<br>Filling of Holy Spirit, Eph. 5:18 |
| Bread, John 6:51 | Pure life, 1 Cor. 5:8<br>Communion, 1 Cor. 11:23–25 |
| Intercessor, John 17; Heb 7:25 | Prayer, Luke 18:1<br>Worship, John 4:24 |
| Veil, Heb. 10:19 | Draw near to God, Heb.10.19–22 |
| Word of God, John 1:1<br>Bread of Heaven, John 6:48<br>Fruitful Branch, Isa.4:2 | Living tablets, 2 Cor. 3:3<br>Feed on Christ's words, John 8:31–32<br>Fruitfulness, John 15:1–16; Gal. 5:22–23 |
| Mercy Seat, Rom. 3:25 | Experience God's mercy, Heb. 4:16 |

# National Distributors

**UK: (and countries not listed below)**
CWR, Waverley Abbey House, Waverley Lane, Farnham, Surrey GU9 8EP.
Tel: (01252) 784710 Outside UK (44) 1252 784710

**AUSTRALIA:** CMC Australasia, PO Box 519, Belmont, Victoria 3216.
Tel: (03) 5241 3288

**CANADA:** CMC Distribution Ltd, PO Box 7000, Niagara on the Lake, Ontario L0S 1JO.
Tel: 1800 325 1297

**GHANA:** Challenge Enterprises of Ghana, PO Box 5723, Accra.
Tel: (021) 222437/223249 Fax: (021) 226227

**HONG KONG:** Cross Communications Ltd, 1/F, 562A Nathan Road, Kowloon.
Tel: 2780 1188 Fax: 2770 6229

**INDIA:** Crystal Communications, 10-3-18/4/1, East Marredpally, Secunderabad – 500 026.
Tel/Fax: (040) 7732801

**KENYA:** Keswick Bookshop, PO Box 10242, Nairobi.
Tel: (02) 331692/226047 Fax: (02) 728557

**MALAYSIA:** Salvation Book Centre (M) Sdn Bhd, 23 Jalan SS 2/64,
47300 Petaling Jaya, Selangor.
Tel: (03) 78766411/78766797 Fax: (03) 78757066/78756360

**NEW ZEALAND:** CMC Australasia, PO Box 36015, Lower Hutt.
Tel: 0800 449 408 Fax: 0800 449 049

**NIGERIA:** FBFM, Helen Baugh House, 96 St Finbarr's College Road, Akoka, Lagos.
Tel: (01) 7747429/4700218/825775/827264

**PHILIPPINES:** OMF Literature Inc, 776 Boni Avenue, Mandaluyong City.
Tel: (02) 531 2183 Fax: (02) 531 1960

**REPUBLIC OF IRELAND:** Scripture Union, 40 Talbot Street, Dublin 1.
Tel: (01) 8363764

**SINGAPORE:** Armour Publishing Pte Ltd, Block 203A Henderson Road,
11–06 Henderson Industrial Park, Singapore 159546.
Tel: 276 9976 Fax: 276 7564

**SOUTH AFRICA:** Struik Christian Books, 80 MacKenzie Street,
PO Box 1144, Cape Town 8000.
Tel: (021) 462 4360 Fax: (021) 461 3612

**SRI LANKA:** Christombu Books, 27 Hospital Street, Colombo 1.
Tel: (01) 433142/328909

**TANZANIA:** CLC Christian Book Centre, PO Box 1384, Mkwepu Street, Dar es Salaam.
Tel/Fax: (022) 2119439

**USA:** CMC Distribution, PO Box 644, Lewiston, New York, 14092-0644.
Tel: 1800 325 1297

**ZIMBABWE:** Word of Life Books, Shop 4, Memorial Building,
35 S Machel Avenue, Harare.
Tel: (04) 781305 Fax: (04) 774739

**For email addresses, visit the CWR website: www.cwr.org.uk**

## Cover to Cover Bible Study Guides

These exciting new study guides from the *Cover to Cover* range have been created to provide a unique resource for group and individual study sessions lasting between one and two hours.

The seven stimulating sessions in each title include opening icebreakers, Bible references, discussion starters and suggestions for personal application. There is an introduction that sets the topic in context as well as helpful notes for group leaders.

**The Image of God**
His Attributes and Character
**ISBN:** 1-85345-228-9

**The Tabernacle**
Entering into God's Presence
**ISBN:** 1-85345-230-0

**The Uniqueness of our Faith**
What makes Christianity Distinctive?
**ISBN:** 1-85345-232-7

**Ruth**
Loving Kindness in Action
**ISBN:** 1-85345-231-9

**Mark**
Life as it is Meant to be Lived
**ISBN:** 1-85345-233-5

**Ephesians**
Claiming your Inheritance
**ISBN:** 1-85345-229-7

**£3.49** each